COOKING
THE
GERMAN
WAY

Copyright © 2003 by Lerner Publications Company

Lerner Publications Company
A division of Lerner Publishing Group
241 First Avenue North
Minneapolis, MN 55401 U.S.A.

Website address: www.lernerbooks.com

Library of Congress Cataloging-in-Publication Data

Parnell, Helga.
    Cooking the German way / by Helga Parnell.— Rev. and expanded.
        p.   cm. — (Easy menu ethnic cookbooks)
    Summary: An introduction to the cooking of Germany featuring such
traditional recipes as spaetzle, hot potato salad, Black Forest torte, and
marzipan. Also includes information on the history, geography, customs
and people of this European country.
    ISBN: 0–8225–4107–6 (lib. bdg. : alk. paper)
    1. Cookery, German—Juvenile literature. 2. Germany—Social life and
customs—Juvenile literature. [1. Cookery, German. 2. Germany—Social
life and customs.] I. Title. II. Series.
TX721 .P27 2003
641.5943—dc21   2002000949

Manufactured in the United States of America
1 2 3 4 5 6 – JR – 08 07 06 05 04 03

easy menu ethnic cookbooks

COOKING

revised and expanded

THE

to include new low-fat

GERMAN

and vegetarian recipes

WAY

Helga Parnell

Lerner Publications Company • Minneapolis

Contents

Introduction

Germans often talk about *die Kunst des guten Kochens*, which means "the art of good cooking." Cooking is indeed an art in Germany. The most important ingredients a German cook can put into a recipe are love, time, patience, and imagination. To this he or she adds only the freshest meats, dairy products, vegetables, fruits, and bakery goods. The result, whether a simple family supper or a holiday feast, is a delicious meal for friends and family to enjoy.

Germany is once again one nation, its division after World War II (1939–1945) having ended in 1990. Throughout the country, food choices reflect the meats, vegetables, and fruits produced locally. Beef, pork, and fish appear often on German tables. Many types of wurst (sausage) are enjoyed, some being the specialty of only one community. Favorites from the country's fertile gardens are potatoes, cabbage, and onions, and apples, plums, and cherries.

Food experts divide German cuisine geographically. In the south, the food is somewhat lighter, like the food of neighbors Austria and Italy. In central Germany, where forests cover the hills, the food is heavy and rich. The food choices of northern Germany are influenced by the sea and by neighboring Scandinavia.

With its hearty sausages and roasts, savory dumplings and spaetzle, and rich pastries and tortes, Germany has long been known for its delicious cuisine. This book will introduce you to German food and traditions.

Both tasty and lucky, New Year's pork and kraut is thought to bring wealth in the coming year. (Recipe on page 62.)

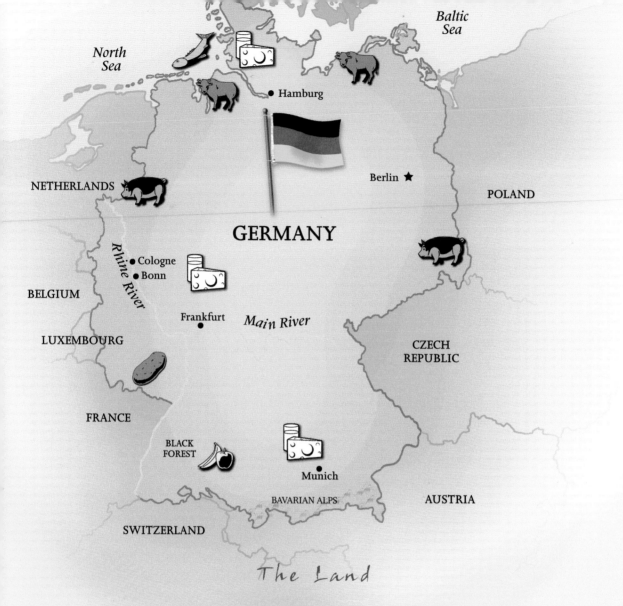

North
Sea

Baltic
Sea

• Hamburg

GERMANY

Berlin ★

NETHERLANDS

POLAND

Rhine River

• Cologne
• Bonn

BELGIUM

Frankfurt
•

Main River

LUXEMBOURG

CZECH
REPUBLIC

FRANCE

BLACK
FOREST

Munich
•

BAVARIAN ALPS

AUSTRIA

SWITZERLAND

The Land

Germany is in the north-central part of Europe. Its 81 million people live in an area somewhat smaller than the state of Montana. The country contains both busy cities and quiet farmlands. A part of the famed Alps Mountains is in the state of Bavaria. In fact, the highest point in Germany is the Zugspitze in the Bavarian Alps. A cogwheel train takes visitors all the way to its snowcapped peak, 9,721 feet above sea level. The view from the train is breathtaking, and in the summer, passengers can see delicate flowers like edelweiss and Alpine rose clinging to the rugged cliffs.

To the west of Bavaria is the Schwarzwald—the Black Forest. This mountainous region is covered with dark forests of evergreen trees. Tradition is strong in the Black Forest, and many of its people still make their living selling handmade crafts, including toys, musical instruments, and cuckoo clocks.

The Rhine-Main River area in western Germany has such major cities as Frankfurt and Bonn, as well as tiny picturesque villages. The Rhine River has cut deep gorges into the land, and in many places, castles built on top of the cliffs tower over the water. Central Germany is also fairy-tale country. Jakob and Wilhelm Grimm were born near Frankfurt. Inspired by the area's beauty, the brothers used it as the setting for their famous fairy tales.

Northwestern Germany is a low, flat area that borders on the North Sea. There are ports in this region that have connected the Germans with the rest of the world since the 1500s.

Throughout Germany there is a strong sense of history. To this day, historic pageants and festivals take place in towns and villages in all parts of the country. Each region has its own special traditions, but everywhere there is a feeling of *Gemütlichkeit*, which is a warm friendliness to both friends and strangers.

The Food

Although there is a nationwide German cuisine, there are some regions in Germany that have their own special cooking traditions. Bavaria is known for its especially hearty meals. Pork roast, served with either potato dumplings or bread dumplings, is popular in nearly every Bavarian home. Even within Bavaria, there are counties with their own culinary specialties. For instance, trout is often served in the Bavarian county of Fränkische Schweiz, where ice-cold streams offer an abundant supply of the delicious fish.

The Brandenburg Gate, completed in 1791, stands just west of downtown Berlin.

In Swabia, a region just west of Bavaria, the specialty is spaetzle, a kind of noodle that can be served with almost any dish. A marinated beef pot roast called sauerbraten is popular throughout Germany, except in the Rhine River area. The dish associated with the coal and iron mining region in the northwestern section of Germany is a robust meat and vegetable stew called *Eintopf*. The miners often take Eintopf, which means "one pot," to work for lunch because it is an entire meal that is easy to carry and is nutritious and filling.

There was a time after World War II when Germans turned away from traditional German cuisine. To celebrate their recovery from the war years, when food was scarce, the Germans created a new, very rich style of cooking. It wasn't long, however, before people began to realize that the delicious new dishes were not very healthy. This led to a wonderful combination of the best of both the old and the new styles of German cooking.

Holidays and Festivals

German families enter as wholeheartedly into holidays and festivals as they do into their everyday tasks. Parents and grandparents happily pass along the traditions and rituals of the special days that dot the German calendar.

Every year on the first Sunday of Advent—the time including the four Sundays just before Christmas—many Christian families set out an *Adventskranz*, an Advent wreath. An Advent wreath is a circle of evergreen branches. It is decorated with four red candles—one for each Sunday in Advent. The wreath may be hung from the ceiling with red ribbons or placed in the center of the dinner table. Every Sunday until Christmas, families gather to sing Christmas carols as a new candle is lit.

German children sometimes count down the days before Christmas with an Advent calendar. An Advent calendar is a colorful calendar with little doors to open, one for every day in December until Christmas. Behind each door is a little surprise that makes the waiting easier.

The first week of December is often an especially busy time. During this time, the cook of the family does all the Christmas baking. Cookies, including the little peppernuts, are prepared. Rich *Lebkuchen* (gingerbread) and *Christstollen* (a special Christmas bread) are also baked and stored for holiday feasting. And, on December 4, Saint Barbara's Day, apple or cherry twigs are set out in a vase of warm water so they will bloom in time for Christmas. Best of all is the eve of December 6. This is the night Saint Nikolaus comes.

A light covering of snow adds a festive air to the holidays in the town of Schwarzenburg.

Saint Nikolaus has a white beard, and he dresses in long robes. German children believe he has a big book that tells him who has been good and who has not. Saint Nikolaus leaves gifts of gingerbread, apples, and nuts to children who have been well behaved. Those who have been naughty must promise to do better in the coming year.

A visit to the Christmas market is another happy December event. At the colorful market, families may buy marzipan candies, cookies (which Germans call biscuits), holiday decorations, toys, and even trees. Sometimes children visiting the market will be treated to a prune man, a figure with a body of prunes and features made with raisins and nuts. Another favorite activity at the Christmas market is choosing the big heart- or star-shaped cookie, decorated and hung on a ribbon, that the child will wear home and then hang on the Christmas tree.

After a long month of preparation, Christmas finally comes. Christmas Eve is a magical night. Many families go to midnight church services. As people walk through the streets to church, the chilly night air is filled with the sound of church bells ringing. Sometimes the first snow of the season falls on Christmas Eve. When families return home from church, they are surprised to find that the Christkindl has been there while they were gone. Christkindl, who is part angel and all mystery, has left presents for everyone. And the Tannenbaum, the lovely decorated Christmas tree, which parents, grandparents, or both have trimmed behind locked—and taped closed—doors, is revealed. To extend the suspense of the waiting gifts, parents expect children to sing a carol or two—"Silent Night" or "Oh, Christmas Tree"—before opening the packages.

On Christmas Day, families gather for their traditional Christmas dinner. Roast goose with vegetables and potato dumplings is a favorite menu. If there is a hunter in the family, the main course might be roast venison. And Christmas is not over on December 25. On December 26, friends and relatives come to talk and eat and admire the tree.

After the excitement and long preparations of Christmas, New Year's Day comes very quickly. Families hope for some fun in the snow. After sledding, skating, or skiing, they return home for pork and kraut. Those who eat this time-honored combination expect to have plenty of money during the year.

Easter is a joyous time. It marks both the coming of spring and

Diners in an outdoor café relax beneath the towering spires of the Cologne Cathedral.

the Christian belief of Jesus rising from the grave. It is a most welcome celebration, coming as it does after the long season of penitence called Lent. In some communities, people light an Easter fire at sunrise, about 6:00 A.M. This roaring outdoor fire with its bright light stands for the victory of light over darkness (which stands for death). People bring candles and light them at the fire. Easter church services and a bountiful Easter breakfast follow.

Children hunt for Easter eggs, supposedly hidden by the Easter bunny. In the Rhineland, lucky children receive Easter manikins, sweet dough in the shapes of little men holding eggs. The manikins are treats for Easter breakfast. Easter dinner centers around lamb, a roast or a lamb meat loaf, shared with family and friends. Families that enjoy painting Easter eggs will display them on a large Easter bouquet. The beautiful eggs are hung on twigs, then placed in the living room for all to admire. Easter Monday rounds out the holiday, with parents relaxing at home, and children playing with friends.

Like Easter, Pentecost, seven Sundays later, is a two-day Christian holiday. One popular Pentecost festival is the Bratwurst Festival in Ochsenfurt on the Main River. Besides feasting on big brats, festival-goers watch a horseback procession to Saint Wolfgang's chapel.

During the summer, Germans and visitors to Germany enjoy all sorts of festivals. In Straubling there is a children's feast, the Kinderzeche. In Oberammergau, the entire community works together to present its Passion Play, performed every ten years. The daylong play tells the story of Jesus' death and includes a long midday break which allows those attending to have both a full dinner and a little nap. In Bamberg a festival called Fischterstechen honors fishers.

Oktoberfest in Munich is a huge festival. Despite its name, it is usually in September. People—some five million—come from all over the world. They sit at long tables under big tents eating, drinking beer, chatting, and listening to lively music. Oktoberfest fare includes roast oxen, smoked tenderloin, fried fish, ham hocks, grilled chicken, bratwust, spareribs, sauerkraut, hot German potato salad, coleslaw, dark breads, and pretzels. The sixteen-day party dates to 1811 when people gathered to celebrate the first wedding anniversary of Crown Prince Ludwig and Princess Theresa. Most German families spend a day at the festival, with everyone touring the massive fairgrounds. After going on some of the exciting rides, parents and children head to the food stands for steaming sausages, all sorts of sandwiches, ice cream, cold drinks, and the fairtime favorite, cotton candy.

Many a church in rural Germany puts on a yearly fair, a kirchweih, on the feast day of the church's patron saint. Young and old gather to dance, drink, and, of course, eat. Goose, fruit kuchen, and doughnuts are among the choices at the food stalls. Whether at a daylong fair at a church in a German village or the weeks-long Oktoberfest, Germans know how to enjoy themselves.

Before You Begin

Cooking any dish, plain or fancy, is easier and more fun if you are familiar with its ingredients and the method of preparation. German cooking makes use of some ingredients that you may not know. Sometimes special cookware is also used, although the recipes in this book can easily be prepared with ordinary utensils and pans.

The most important thing you need to know before you start is how to be a careful cook. On the following page, you'll find a few rules that will make your cooking experience safe, fun, and easy. Next, take a look at the "dictionary" of terms and special ingredients. You may also want to read the list of tips on preparing healthy, low-fat meals for yourself, your family, and your friends.

Once you've picked out a recipe to try, read through it from beginning to end. Now you are ready to shop for ingredients and to organize the pans and utensils you will need. When you have assembled everything, you're ready to begin cooking.

Beef rolls in cream sauce are a delicious choice for holidays and special occasions. (Recipe on pages 32–33.)

The Careful Cook

Whenever you cook, there are certain safety rules you must always keep in mind. Even experienced cooks follow these rules when they are in the kitchen.

- Always wash your hands before handling food.
- Thoroughly wash all raw vegetables and fruits to remove dirt, chemicals and insecticides.
- Use a cutting board when cutting up vegetables and fruits. Don't cut them up in your hand! And be sure to cut in a direction *away* from you and your fingers.
- Long hair or loose clothing can easily catch fire if brought near the burners of a stove. If you have long hair, tie it back before you start cooking.
- Turn all pot handles toward the back of the stove so that you will not catch your sleeve or jewelry on them. This is especially important when younger brothers and sisters are around. They could easily knock off a pot and get burned.
- Always use a pot holder to steady hot pots or to take pans out of the oven. Don't use a wet cloth on a hot pan because the steam it produces could burn you.
- Lift the lid of a steaming pot with the opening away from you so that you will not get burned.
- If you get burned, hold the burn under cold running water. Do not put grease or butter on it. Cold water helps to take the heat out, but grease or butter will only keep it in.
- If grease or cooking oil catches fire, throw baking soda or salt at the bottom of the flame to put it out. (Water will not put out a grease fire.) Call for help and try to turn all the stove burners to "off."

Cooking Utensils

ramekin—An individual baking dish that is 3 to 4 inches in diameter

slotted spoon—A spoon with small openings in the bowl. It is used to lift solid food out of a liquid.

springform pan—A two-part round pan with high sides. A spring on the side releases the rim, so that the food baked inside can easily be served.

Cooking Terms

brown—To cook food quickly over high heat so that the surface turns an even brown

cream—To beat two or more ingredients together until the mixture has a smooth consistency

dust—To sprinkle the surface of something lightly with a powdery ingredient, such as flour or sugar

fold—To blend an ingredient with other ingredients by using a gentle, overturning circular motion

hard-cook—To cook an egg in its shell until both the yolk and white are firm

knead—To work dough using a pressing and folding motion to make it smooth and elastic

marinade—A seasoned liquid in which a food is marinated, or soaked

pinch—A very small amount, usually what you can pick up between your thumb and forefinger

scald—To heat a liquid (such as milk) to a temperature just below its boiling point

sift—To put an ingredient, such as flour or sugar, through a sifter to break up any lumps simmer—To cook over low heat in liquid kept just below its boiling point. Bubbles may occasionally rise to the surface.

stir-fry—To fry quickly over high heat in oil or fat, stirring or turning the food to prevent burning

whip—To beat cream, gelatin mixture, or egg white at high speed until light and fluffy in texture

Special Ingredients

almond extract—A liquid, made from the oil of almonds, that is used to give an almond flavor to food

basil—A rich and fragrant herb whose leaves are used in cooking

bay leaf—The dried leaf of the bay (also called laurel) tree

candied cherries—Sweet cherries that have been cooked in a sugar syrup

caraway seed—A strongly flavored seed used in making breads and cheeses

cardamom—An fragrant spice with a spicy sweet flavor

chives—A member of the onion family whose thin, green stalks are chopped and used as a garnish and a flavoring

cloves—Dried buds from a small evergreen tree. Cloves can be used whole or ground to flavor food.

cod—Freshwater fish with lean, firm flesh that is widely available and frequently served

coriander—A pungent herb whose leaves and seeds are both used for seasoning. The seeds are ground and used to flavor German foods such as frankfurters and baked goods.

currants—Seedless, dried Zante grapes, which look like tiny, dark raisins

Dijon-style mustard—A commercially prepared condiment (ingredient used to enhance the flavor of food) made from mustard seed, white wine, vinegar, salt, and other spices

dill weed—An aromatic herb whose seeds and leaves are both used in cooking

golden raisins—Dried white grapes often used in fruitcakes and breads

marzipan—Almond paste and sugar mixed to form a soft, easy to shape mixture. Marzipan is used for making desserts and colorful, decorative candies.

mustard seed—The pungent seed of the mustard plant, which is used to flavor food

nutmeg—A fragrant spice, either whole or ground, that is often used in desserts

oregano—The dried leaves, whole or ground, of a rich and fragrant herb that is used as a seasoning in cooking

parsnip—The long, white, sweet-tasting root vegetable of the parsnip plant

paste color—Food coloring in the form of a soft paste which produces vivid colors and does not thin out dough as liquid food coloring does

slivered almonds—Almonds that have been split into thin strips

Thuringer—Sausage seasoned with coriander. It originated in the German region called Thuringia.

thyme—A fragrant herb used fresh or dried to season food

whitefish—Member of the salmon family, named for its firm, white flesh. It is high in fat and mild in flavor.

Healthy and Low-Fat Cooking Tips

Many cooks are concerned about preparing healthy, low-fat meals. First of all, healthy meals include lots of vegetables and fruits. Nutrition experts recommend eating a total of five servings of vegetables and fruits each day. You can choose fresh, frozen, canned, or dried fruits and vegetables. These foods are both low in fat and high in vitamins, minerals, and fiber. Second, there are simple ways to trim fat from foods that are high in fat. Here are some tips for adapting the recipes in this book.

Beef and pork may be heavily marbled with fat. For recipes calling for meat, use a sharp knife to cut off excess fat. Also, in the past, cooks used four ounces (¼ lb.) of meat per serving. But three ounces per portion is usually enough. If you want to be sure that the amount of food for each person is generous, increase the amount of vegetables instead of the meat.

Many recipes call for butter or oil to sauté onion, garlic, green pepper, and other ingredients. Using oil lowers saturated fat right away, but you can also reduce the amount of oil you use. Sprinkling a little salt on the vegetables brings out their natural juices, so less oil is needed. It's also a good idea to use a nonstick frying pan if you decide to use less oil than the recipe calls for. Using olive oil instead of other vegetable oils also makes the dish healthier.

Dairy products are a common source of unwanted fat. You can use low-fat or fat-free sour cream in place of regular sour cream successfully. The same goes for reduced fat versions of cheese, cream cheese, and milk. When a recipe calls for cream or half-and-half, try substituting fat-free half-and-half or canned evaporated skim milk.

There are many ways to prepare meals that are good for you and taste great. As you become a more experienced cook, try experimenting with recipes and substitutions to find the methods that work best for you.

METRIC CONVERSIONS

Cooks in the United States measure both liquid and solid ingredients using standard containers based on the 8-ounce cup and the tablespoon. These measurements are based on volume, while the metric system of measurement is based on both weight (for solids) and volume (for liquids). To convert from U.S. fluid tablespoons, ounces, quarts, and so forth to metric liters is a straightforward conversion, using the chart below. However, since solids have different weights—one cup of rice does not weigh the same as one cup of grated cheese, for example—many cooks who use the metric system have kitchen scales to weigh different ingredients. The chart below will give you a good starting point for basic conversions to the metric system.

MASS (weight)

1 ounce (oz.)	=	28.0 grams (g)
8 ounces	=	227.0 grams
1 pound (lb.) or 16 ounces	=	0.45 kilograms (kg)
2.2 pounds	=	1.0 kilogram

LIQUID VOLUME

1 teaspoon (tsp.)	=	5.0 milliliters (ml)
1 tablespoon (tbsp.)	=	15.0 milliliters
1 fluid ounce (oz.)	=	30.0 milliliters
1 cup (c.)	=	240 milliliters
1 pint (pt.)	=	480 milliliters
1 quart (qt.)	=	0.95 liters (l)
1 gallon (gal.)	=	3.80 liters

LENGTH

¼ inch (in.)	=	0.6 centimeters (cm)
½ inch	=	1.25 centimeters
1 inch	=	2.5 centimeters

TEMPERATURE

212°F	=	100°C (boiling point of water)
225°F	=	110°C
250°F	=	120°C
275°F	=	135°C
300°F	=	150°C
325°F	=	160°C
350°F	=	180°C
375°F	=	190°C
400°F	=	200°C

(To convert temperature in Fahrenheit to Celsius, subtract 32 and multiply by .56)

PAN SIZES

8-inch cake pan	=	20 x 4-centimeter cake pan
9-inch cake pan	=	23 x 3.5-centimeter cake pan
11 x 7-inch baking pan	=	28 x 18-centimeter baking pan
13 x 9-inch baking pan	=	32.5 x 23-centimeter baking pan
9 x 5-inch loaf pan	=	23 x 13-centimeter loaf pan
2-quart casserole	=	2-liter casserole

A German Table

Just as German cooks take pride in the quality and variety of their foods, so they take pride in the visual appeal of their table. First comes the carefully ironed tablecloth and napkins. Then the table is set with pretty flower-patterned dishes and gleaming tableware. Because Germany is home to several world-famous china manufacturers, well-to-do families may have several sets of lovely dishes. On special occasions, such as birthdays, heirloom platters and bowls, inherited from generations past, are part of the table setting.

Bread baskets or boards hold the rolls and loaves that Germans love. The breakfast table always features a bowl of jam or jelly, preferably homemade. The dinner and supper tables always have a glass dish piled with pickles—the popular dill pickle or a selection of mixed pickles—mushrooms, cubed squash, little gherkins, or perhaps walnuts. Drinking glasses might be mugs for beer in the southern part of the country or stemmed glasses for wine in the northern part, along with milk glasses for children. Little vases of garden flowers are often found on the dining table in the summer.

Eating outdoors is the perfect way to enjoy a German dinner.

A German Menu

A German breakfast, which is eaten between 7:00 and 8:00 A.M., is quite small, usually just rolls and coffee or milk. Sometimes, however, eggs, granola with yogurt, or fruit with a cheese similar to ricotta, called *quark*, are served. On Sundays, some people also have a second breakfast. Second breakfast is eaten at about 10:30 or 11:00 A.M.. and is made up of something simple like cheese and crackers and apple juice.

Below are menu plans for a typical German dinner and supper along with lists of the ingredients necessary to prepare these meals. Germans generally don't eat dessert after a meal, although fruit is sometimes served. The wonderful pastries for which Germany is famous are eaten as an afternoon snack with coffee, tea, or milk.

DINNER

Clear beef broth

Pork roast

Potato dumplings

Asparagus

SHOPPING LIST:

Produce

garlic (or garlic powder)
½ small carrot
tops of 2 stalks celery
2½ lb. potatoes
1½ lb. asparagus
3 onions
parsley

Dairy/Egg/Meat

1 lb. beef chuck
2- to 3-lb. rolled pork loin
1 c. milk
butter or margarine
½ lb. beef bones (optional)

Canned/Bottled/Boxed

cornstarch
vegetable oil

Miscellaneous

bay leaves
salt
pepper
1 slice white bread
nutmeg
thyme
flour

SUPPER

Open-faced sandwiches

Potato soup

Apple cake

SHOPPING LIST:

Produce

2 medium carrots
6 medium potatoes
1 parsnip
2 stalks celery
1 large onion, white or
    yellow
1 red onion
1 medium tomato
1 medium cucumber
lettuce or leaf spinach
1 lemon
4 medium tart apples

Dairy/Egg/Meat

½ lb. cold cuts (salami,
    bologna, ham, or
    Thuringer)
½ lb. cheese (Swiss, cheddar,
    Muenster, or Colby)
1 ham bone or smoked pork
    hock
4 eggs
butter or margarine
whipping cream

Canned/Bottled/Boxed

baby dill pickles or gherkins
6 c. chicken broth
pimento-stuffed olives

Miscellaneous

rye bread
salt
pepper
sugar
flour
baking powder
cinnamon

Dinner / Mittagessen

Germans have traditionally eaten their biggest meal of the day—dinner—at about noon. But these days, most Germans work outside of the home, so dinner is served at night during the week, and the noon meal is usually just a sandwich. On the weekends, however, dinner is still served at the traditional time.

Dinner is a hearty meal that usually starts with soup, especially if it's a festive dinner. This is followed by some sort of meat—usually a roast. Pork is served most often. Beef, poultry such as goose, and game including venison are well liked too. The meat is served with potatoes, spaetzle, or dumplings; a salad; and one or two kinds of vegetables. Colorful vegetables such as juicy red tomatoes, white cauliflower, green cabbage, tender mushrooms, and both green and white asparagus are abundant in Germany. These healthy vegetables may be served alone or in delicious combinations. If dessert is served, it is likely to be very light, usually just fruit or a small dish of pudding or ice cream.

Pork roast (bottom, recipe on page 30) served with spaetzle (top, recipe on page 31) makes a savory meal.

Pork Roast/ Schweinebraten

The meat juices from this dish can be served as a clear gravy with potato dumplings or spaetzle.

1 2- to 3-lb. rolled pork loin

1 tsp. salt

½ tsp. pepper

½ tsp. garlic powder, or 2 cloves garlic, peeled and crushed

½ tsp. dried thyme

1 bay leaf

2 medium onions, peeled and chopped

2 c. water

1. Preheat oven to 325°F. Rub pork with salt, pepper, garlic, thyme, and crumbled bay leaf.

2. Place pork with the fat side up on rack in shallow roasting pan. If you have a meat thermometer, insert it so tip is in center of thickest part of meat. Thermometer should not touch fat or bone. Surround meat with onions.

3. Roast 33 to 38 minutes per pound, or until meat thermometer registers 165°F.

4. Remove roast from oven. Add water and place a loose tent of heavy-duty aluminum foil over roast. Let stand 15 to 20 minutes, or until meat thermometer shows 170°F. Standing time makes roast easier to carve.

Preparation time: 10 minutes
Cooking time: about 1 hour 40 minutes
Serves 6 to 8

Spaetzle / Spätzle

Spaetzle is especially popular in the Black Forest region of Germany. It is usually served in place of potatoes or noodles with a roast as part of a filling dinner.

1¾ c. all-purpose flour

1 tsp. salt

2 eggs, beaten

½ to ¾ c. warm water

2 tbsp. butter

1. Sift flour and ½ tsp. salt together into a medium bowl. Make a hollow in the center of flour and add eggs and ¼ c. warm water. Slowly stir the flour into the liquid.

2. Stir in remaining water, little by little, until mixture has the consistency of cookie dough. Beat vigorously with wooden spoon until small bubbles form.

3. Fill a large saucepan half full of water and add ½ tsp. salt. Bring to a boil. Scoop up small pieces of dough with a wet teaspoon and drop into water. Cook only enough spaetzle at a time to fill the pan without touching.

4. Boil, uncovered, for 6 to 8 minutes, or until tender. Remove from water with slotted spoon.

5. When all of spaetzle is done, rinse with cold water and drain well.

6. Just before serving, place spaetzle in medium saucepan with the butter. Cook, stirring constantly, over low heat until butter is melted.

Preparation time: 20 minutes
Cooking time: 30 minutes
Serves 4 to 6

Beef Rolls in Cream Sauce/
Rindsrouladen in Rahmsosse

Rindsrouladen are a favorite Sunday or holiday dish throughout Germany.

4 4 - by 8-inch. slices round steak, ¼-inch. thick, about 1½ lb.*

1 tsp. salt

½ tsp. pepper

4 tsp. Dijon-style mustard

4 slices lean bacon*

½ c. finely chopped onion

1 large dill pickle, cut lengthwise into 4 spears

6 tbsp. all-purpose flour

3 tbsp. vegetable oil

1½ c. hot water

3 tbsp. cream*

1. Place one slice of steak on a sheet of waxed paper and sprinkle lightly with salt and pepper. Spread 1 tsp. of mustard over meat, top with one slice of bacon, and sprinkle with 2 tbsp. onion. Place one pickle spear at one of the 4-inch ends of the meat and roll up meat around it. Secure meat roll with a toothpick. Repeat with remaining slices of meat.

2. Pour 4 tbsp. flour into a shallow dish. Roll each meat roll in flour until completely covered.

3. In a large frying pan, heat oil over medium heat for 2 minutes. Carefully place meat rolls in oil with tongs and cook for about 10 to 15 minutes, or until brown on all sides.

4. Preheat oven to 350°F.

5. Place meat rolls in a roasting pan, add hot water, and cover pan tightly. Cook for 1 to 1½ hours, or until fork-tender.

6. Place meat rolls on a platter. Pour meat juices into a small saucepan and place over medium heat.

7. Slowly sprinkle meat juices with 2 tbsp. flour, stirring constantly. Cook and stir one minute. Remove from heat and stir in cream. Pour cream sauce over meat rolls and serve.

Preparation time: 20 to 30 minutes
Cooking time: 1¼ to 1¾ hours
Serves 4

*To keep fat in this recipe to a minimum, trim steak of any excess fat and use turkey bacon and fat-free half-and-half in place of bacon and cream.

Fish with Mustard Sauce/*Fisch mit Senfsosse*

4 c. water

½ lemon, sliced

I medium onion, peeled and sliced

2 bay leaves

I tbsp. shredded carrot

I tsp. salt

6 peppercorns

2 lbs. I-in.-thick fillets of cod, walleye, or any firm whitefish

mustard sauce (recipe follows)

1. Place water, lemon, onion, bay leaves, carrot, salt, and peppercorns in a wide skillet and bring to a boil over high heat.

2. Add fish, placing fillets in a single layer, and reduce heat to low. Simmer, covered, for 10 minutes, or until fish flakes. Save the cooking liquid to use in the mustard sauce.

3. Place fish on warm platter. Cover with foil to keep warm. Serve with mustard sauce.

Preparation time: 10 minutes
Cooking time: 15 minutes
Serves 8

Mustard Sauce:

2 tbsp. butter, margarine, or vegetable oil

2 tbsp. all-purpose flour

I c. cooking liquid from fish

3 tbsp. Dijon-style mustard

dash of salt

I tsp. sugar

I to 2 tbsp. half-and-half or fat-free half-and-half

1. In a medium saucepan, melt butter over low heat. Sprinkle in flour a little at a time, stirring well after each addition.

2. Stir in liquid from fish a little at a time. Add mustard, salt, and sugar and stir well.

3. Remove from heat and stir in 1 tbsp. half-and-half. Sauce should be creamy and easy to pour. If too thick, stir in another tbsp. of half-and-half.

Preparation time: 5 minutes
Cooking time: 5 minutes
Makes 1 cup; serves 8

Clear Beef Broth / *Klare Fleischbrühe*

Many families start Sunday dinner with this delicious beef broth. The meat from the broth can be sliced and served with mustard sauce (see recipe on page 34) or bottled horseradish sauce and boiled potatoes garnished with parsley.

2 tbsp. vegetable oil

1½ lb. beef chuck, cut into 1½-in. chunks

10 c. water

½ small carrot, finely chopped

tops of 2 stalks celery, finely chopped

1 medium onion, peeled and chopped

½ lb. beef bones (optional)

1 bay leaf

1 to 2 tsp. salt

¼ tsp. pepper

1 tbsp. fresh chopped parsley or chives

½ tsp. nutmeg

1. Heat oil in a large kettle. Cook beef chunks in oil over medium heat until brown on all sides.

2. Add water and heat to boiling. Skim foam from water. Stir in carrot, celery tops, onion, beef bones (if desired), bay leaf, salt, and pepper.

3. Cover, reduce heat to low, and simmer for 3 hours. (Do not boil.)

4. Remove meat and bones from broth. Save the meat. Carefully pour broth through sieve with another large pan underneath to catch liquid. Skim fat from broth.

5. Use broth and beef right away or place beef and broth in separate containers, cover, and refrigerate up to 24 hours.

6. Serve broth hot, sprinkled with parsley or chives, and nutmeg. Also delicious served with potato dumplings. (See recipe on page 38.)

Preparation time: 25 to 35 minutes
Cooking time: 3 hours 15 minutes
Serves 6

Potato Dumplings/*Kartoffelklösse*

2½ lb. potatoes (3 or 4 medium)

1 c. milk

2 tsp. salt

1½ c. cornstarch

1 slice white bread

flour for molding dumplings

1. Wash potatoes well and place in a large saucepan. Cover with water and bring to a boil over high heat. Reduce heat to medium-low and cover, leaving cover slightly ajar to let steam escape. Cook for 20 to 25 minutes, or until potatoes can be easily pierced with a fork. Drain.

2. Peel potatoes as soon as they are cool enough to handle, and grate through largest holes of a grater.

3. In a saucepan, scald milk over medium heat. Add milk, 1 tsp. salt, and cornstarch to potatoes and stir well. Set aside for 15 minutes.

4. Toast bread. Cut into ½-inch cubes.

5. With clean, lightly floured hands, form dough into 3-inch balls. Press two or three cubes of toast into center of each ball. Reshape balls.

6. Fill a large kettle half full of water, add 1 tsp. salt, and bring to a boil. Reduce heat to low and, with a slotted spoon, carefully place dumplings in water. Do not cover. Simmer 20 to 30 minutes, or until dumplings float. Remove dumplings with slotted spoon. Serve hot.

Cooking time for potatoes: 25 minutes
Preparation time for dumplings: 25 to 30 minutes
Cooking time for dumplings: 20 to 30 minutes
Makes 8 dumplings

Asparagus / Spargel

Asparagus is very popular in the spring when it is at its peak of perfection, tender and flavorful. German cooks plan ½ lb. of asparagus per person as a side dish. Restaurants offer springtime "Spargel" menus featuring favorite asparagus dishes, both hot and cold.

1½ lb. asparagus spears*

1 to 2 tbsp. butter or margarine

1. Snap off tough ends of asparagus spears as far down as spears snap easily, and discard ends. Wash asparagus by plunging into a container of cold water. Lift out and drain. Leave spears whole.

2. Place spears in a wide frying pan. Pour 1 inch of water into pan. Cook over low to medium heat 6 to 8 minutes, until crisp-tender.

3. Drain asparagus. Add butter. Serve promptly.

Preparation time: 10 to 15 minutes
Cooking time: 8 minutes
Serves 6

*If asparagus is very sandy, wash in cold water, then tear off the little points on the stem to get rid of the sand under them. Some cooks recommend peeling asparagus stems with a vegetable peeler for maximum tenderness.

One-Pot Meal with Chicken/*Eintopf mit Huhn*

Eintopf can also be made with beef or lamb. If you choose beef, use round or rump. If you choose lamb, use shank or shoulder. Beef or lamb will need to be cooked 45 minutes before adding the vegetables.

I tbsp. butter, margarine, or vegetable oil

I medium onion, peeled and chopped

3 tbsp. finely chopped celery tops

I lb. boneless light or dark chicken meat, cut into bite-sized pieces*

2¼ c. water

2 medium potatoes

4 medium carrots

¼ head cabbage

2½ c. cut green beans, fresh or frozen

I medium tomato

I tsp. salt

½ tsp. pepper

2 tbsp. fresh chopped parsley

1. In a large kettle, melt butter over medium-high heat. Add onion and celery tops and stir-fry until onion is transparent.

2. Add meat and brown lightly, 10 to 15 minutes. Add ¼ c. water.

3. Cover pan, reduce heat to medium-low and cook until meat is tender, about 15 minutes.

4. Meanwhile, peel potatoes and carrots. Keeping vegetables separate, cut potatoes, carrots, cabbage, and tomato into bite-sized pieces.

5. Atop the meat, make a layer of potatoes, then carrots, then cabbage, then green beans, then tomato. Add 2 c. water, salt, and pepper. Cover and simmer over low heat for about 25 to 30 minutes, or until vegetables are tender.

6. Sprinkle with parsley and serve.

Preparation time: 20 to 30 minutes
Cooking time: 35 to 45 minutes
Serves 4 to 6

*For an all-vegetable one-pot, omit the meat and add ¼ head cauliflower, broken into florets; 1 leek, well washed and sliced; and 1 c. fresh or frozen green peas.

Red Cabbage/ Rotkohl

This tangy, bright-colored side dish is delicious with beef, pork, or wild game. It does not go well with chicken or fish. The vinegar, with its natural acid, preserves the vivid color of the red cabbage. Leftover red cabbage can be chilled and served as a salad.

2 strips bacon, diced*

1 medium onion, peeled and chopped

10 to 12 c. shredded red cabbage (about 2⅓ lb. cabbage)

1 medium tart apple, cored and chopped (no need to peel)

4 to 5 whole cloves

2 bay leaves

½ tsp. salt

⅛ tsp. pepper

¼ cup red wine vinegar

1. In a large saucepan, fry bacon over medium heat until almost crisp. Add onions and stir-fry until transparent.

2. Add cabbage and stir well. Add remaining ingredients and stir again.

3. Cover and simmer over low heat for 1 hour, or until cabbage is tender. If possible, remove whole cloves before serving.

Preparation time: 20 minutes
Cooking time: 1 hour
Serves 6 to 8

*If you prefer not to use bacon in this side dish, use 2 tbsp. butter or oil for cooking the onions.

Rotkohl's lively color and unique blend of flavors make it an exciting side dish or salad.

Supper / Abendessen

On days when dinner is eaten at noon, the evening meal is a very simple, light supper served at 5:30 or 6:00 P.M. Supper usually consists of sandwiches or a thick soup or salad. The sandwiches would be made with excellent bakery breads—dark pumpernickel rye or one of the many wonderful whole-grain breads. Along with these delicious breads would go the famed Westphalian ham or the hundreds of kinds of wurst (sausages), cheeses such as Muenster, fresh greens, and sliced tomatoes.

Many of the filling supper soups combine common foods, such as beans and frankfurters, tomatoes and chicken broth, or potatoes and cucumber. A cubed beef and green pepper soup is called goulash.

During warm weather, salads make good suppers. There are many versions of the beloved potato salad. One tangy potato salad is seasoned with a cooked dressing made with beer. Other favorite salads include cabbage with apples, red beets, green beans with onion, herring with sour cream, and fruit with walnuts.

A supper that is popular with children is potato pancakes. These pancakes are made with grated potato and topped with applesauce.

There is no reason to cover up these delightfully garnished open-faced sandwiches. (Recipe on page 46.)

Open-Faced Sandwiches/*Belegte Brote*

These sandwiches are equally delicious without the cold cuts. Instead of meat, use additional vegetables, such as canned asparagus spears, pickled beet slices, and cut marinated artichoke hearts. Plan plenty of time when you arrange these sandwiches so that each one will be attractive.

½ lb. cold cuts (salami, bologna, ham, or Thuringer)

½ lb. cheese (Swiss, cheddar, Muenster, or Colby), sliced

2 hard-cooked eggs, shelled and sliced into thin rounds*

1 red onion, peeled and sliced

1 medium tomato, sliced, or 6 cherry tomatoes, halved

½ cucumber, sliced

baby pickles (dill or gherkin)

pimento-stuffed olives

lettuce or leaf spinach

6 to 8 slices rye bread

butter or margarine

*To hard-cook eggs, place in saucepan and cover with cold water to 1 inch above eggs. Cook over medium-high heat, uncovered, until boiling. Remove from heat, cover, and let stand 18 minutes. Drain off hot water and cover eggs with cold water. Tap eggs to crack shells, then chill until ready to use.

1. Bring cold cuts, cheese, eggs, onions, tomatoes, cucumber, pickles, olives, and lettuce to room temperature, so that ingredients will taste their best when sandwiches are served.

2. Spread bread lightly with butter, making sure to get it to the very edge. Cover butter with leaf of lettuce.

3. Make a different arrangement of meat, cheese, egg slices, vegetables, and garnishes on each slice of bread. On one sandwich you might start with a slice of cheese, and then arrange a cold cut or two atop the cheese, shaping the cold cut into a cornucopia or folding it into a triangle. Another sandwich could have the cold cut laid flat as the base of the sandwich, with alternating pieces of cheese and egg slices diagonally across the meat. Garnish each sandwich attractively with your choice of onion, tomato, cucumber, pickles, and/or olives.

4. These sandwiches are eaten with knife and fork.

Preparation time: 30 minutes
Serves 4 to 6

Potato Soup / *Kartoffelsuppe*

This filling soup has a light gold color due to the carrots cooked with the potatoes. If you are in a hurry, just scrub potatoes and carrots thoroughly, then chop.

6 medium potatoes

2 medium carrots

1 large onion

1 medium parsnip (optional)

2 stalks celery

1 ham bone or 1 smoked pork hock*

6 c. chicken broth or water

1 tsp. salt

½ tsp. pepper

1. Peel and cube potatoes.

2. Peel and chop carrots, onion, and parsnip.

3. Chop celery.

4. Place potatoes, carrots, onion, parsnip, celery, ham bone or pork hock, broth, salt, and pepper in a large kettle. Bring to a boil over high heat. Reduce heat to low, cover, and simmer 20 to 30 minutes, or until vegetables are tender.

5. Carefully pour soup through a large sieve with another pan underneath to catch liquid. Remove ham bone.

6. With a large spoon, press the vegetables through the sieve into soup. You can also mash vegetables into the broth with a potato masher. Stir well.

*To change the recipe to a meatless soup, leave out the ham or pork, use vegetarian broth or water, and sprinkle the finished soup with shredded cheese.

Preparation time: 25 to 30 minutes
Cooking time: 20 to 30 minutes
Serves 4 to 6

Baked Eggs with Cheese/*Eingebackene Eier mit Käse*

This is a simple dish for a light supper or easy brunch.

butter or lowfat vegetable spray

6 slices white bread

enough thin-sliced Swiss cheese to cover bread

6 eggs

6 tbsp. regular or fat-free half-and-half

salt and pepper

1. Heat oven to 375°F.

2. Butter or spray a rectangular baking dish. Cover bottom with bread, placing slices side by side in a single layer.

3. Arrange sliced Swiss cheese atop bread, covering it completely.

4. Break eggs, centering one egg over each slice of bread. Spoon about 1 tbsp. half-and-half over yolk of each egg. Sprinkle with salt and pepper.

5. Bake 15 to 20 minutes, or until eggs are done as desired.

Preparation time: 10 to 15 minutes
Cooking time: 15 to 20 minutes
Serves 6

*For a single serving, grease a single ramekin. Arrange in it one slice bread and one egg with sliced cheese and half-and-half in order given. Bake as directed above.

Baked eggs are a favorite light entrée at any time of the day.

Hot Potato Salad/Warmer Kartoffelsalat

For a vegetarian version of this tangy salad, leave out the bacon and fry the onion in 2 tbsp. vegetable oil.

4 to 5 medium boiling potatoes
(1 ½ lb.), cooked with skin on
(see directions for cooking
potatoes on page 38)

6 slices bacon

½ c. finely chopped onion

4 tbsp. cider vinegar

3 tbsp. water

1 tsp. sugar

½ tsp. salt

¼ tsp. freshly ground pepper

2 tbsp. chopped fresh parsley

1. Peel potatoes and slice thinly.

2. Fry bacon slowly in skillet until brown and crisp, then drain on paper towels. Leave bacon fat in skillet. Crumble bacon when cool.

3. Fry onion in bacon fat, stirring frequently, until transparent and starting to brown.

4. Stir in vinegar, water, sugar, salt, and pepper. Cook, stirring constantly, for a minute or so.

5. Pour hot vinegar mixture over potatoes. Sprinkle in crumbled bacon. With large spoon, stir salad carefully until potato slices are coated with vinegar sauce.

6. Serve hot or at room temperature. Garnish with parsley.

Preparation time: 25 minutes
Cooking time: 15 minutes
Serves 4 to 5

Heaven and Earth/Himmel und Erde

Apples from heaven and potatoes from the earth are often combined in Germany. Though it is usually accompanied by blood sausage or liver, this is a filling meatless main course all on its own. It would be excellent with green beans or green peas as a side dish.

I large onion

I tbsp. butter or margarine

2 c. prepared applesauce

2 c. prepared mashed potatoes*

½ tsp. salt

⅛ tsp. freshly ground black pepper

1. Slice onion in thin slices.

2. Heat butter in a medium saucepan. Fry onion slices in the butter, stirring frequently.

3. Stir applesauce into onion slices. Cook 5 to 10 minutes, stirring often, to thicken applesauce.

4. Stir mashed potatoes into apple mixture. Cook until steaming hot. Season with salt and pepper.

Preparation time: 5 minutes
Cooking time: 20 to 25 minutes
Serves 4 to 6

*This combination can be made with homemade, frozen, or instant mashed potatoes.

Pastries / Gebäck

Gebäck are the fancy pastries, tortes, cakes, and cookies that are such an important part of German cuisine. These desserts are not served after meals, but rather they are eaten as snacks in the afternoon. At 2:30 or 3:30 P.M., the *Konditoreien*, or coffee shops, are filled with people enjoying such wonderful desserts as Black Forest torte and apple cake.

A stop at the coffee shop for a sweet treat is a favorite ending for an afternoon of errands. It is fun to search through the display cases for the perfect pastry, with each person trying a different one. Then everyone settles down with their pastry of choice, a cup of rich coffee for grownups, and hot chocolate or milk for children.

Some of the pastries are so delicious that they have become popular in other countries. One is crumb cake or *Streuselkuchen*, a yeast-raised cake with a crumbly flour-and-butter topping. Another is strawberry Bavarian cream, in which fresh berries are folded into gelatin-thickened whipped cream.

Indulge your midday sweet tooth with a slice of rich Black Forest torte. (Recipe on pages 54–55.)

Black Forest Torte / Schwarzwälder Kirschtorte

This wonderful dessert, which originated in Germany's Black Forest, is popular all over the world.

Cake:

1 18¼-oz. pkg. chocolate cake mix

water, oil, and eggs for preparing
    cake batter as directed on pkg.

Filling and Topping:

21-oz. can cherry pie filling

2 c. whipping cream, chilled

¼ c. powdered sugar

1 tsp. vanilla extract

2 oz. semisweet chocolate or ¼ c.
    chocolate candy sprinkles

12 to 14 maraschino cherries

1. Preheat oven to 350°F. Grease and flour three 9-inch round cake pans.

2. Prepare chocolate cake batter following package directions using water, oil, and eggs.

3. Pour one-third of the batter into each cake pan. Bake for 15 to 20 minutes, or until toothpick inserted in center comes out clean.

4. Let cake cool in pans for 5 minutes. Run a knife around the insides of the pans so cake doesn't stick, and turn out pans onto racks to cool.

5. Place pie filling in a large colander over a bowl the same size. Stir cherries until ½ c. of the thickened cherry liquid has fallen into the bowl. Refrigerate this ½ c. filling for use later as an ice cream topping. Divide cherries and remaining filling into two equal amounts.

6. Put whipping cream, powdered sugar, and vanilla into a medium bowl. Beat with electric mixer or rotary beater until stiff peaks form. Refrigerate until you are ready to assemble the torte.

7. Put one square of chocolate in a warm place for 15 minutes or so while assembling torte. Keep second square of chocolate cool so that it is firm.

8. Place one completely cooled cake layer upside down on a cake plate. Cover with about ¾ c. of whipped cream. Spoon half of cherry filling over whipped cream, spacing cherries evenly. Top with second cake layer. Spread cake with another ¾ c. whipped cream, again putting half the cherry filling over cream. Top with the third cake layer. Frost the side and top of cake with remaining whipped cream.

9. Make chocolate curls from the warm square of chocolate. Hold chocolate in one hand and, with a vegetable peeler in the other hand, carefully slice across chocolate with long strokes to form curls. Grate the firm square of chocolate by running the chocolate over the holes of a hand-held grater.

10. Garnish torte with maraschino cherries, spacing them evenly around the edge of the torte. This is a way of marking the twelve or fourteen servings so that pieces will be the same size. Arrange chocolate curls over top of torte. Pat grated chocolate into whipped cream spread on sides of torte. If using chocolate candy sprinkles, scatter on top and sides of cake. Refrigerate until ready to serve. Refrigerate any leftover torte.

Preparation time: 20 minutes for cake layers,
35 to 40 minutes for assembling torte
Baking time: 15 to 20 minutes
Serves 12 to 14

Apple Cake / Apfelkuchen

You can substitute 1 lb. of cherries, pitted, or twelve prune plums, pitted and quartered, for the apples.

1 lemon

4 medium-sized tart apples*

1 ⅓ c. all-purpose flour

1¼ tsp. baking powder

¼ lb. (½ c.) butter or margarine, softened

½ c. plus 2 tbsp. sugar

2 eggs at room temperature

2 tsp. cinnamon

whipped cream

*Look for one of these varieties of tart apples when making this cake: McIntosh, York Imperial, Granny Smith, Stayman, Newtown Pippin, Winesap, Cortland, Northern Spy, Idared, Gala, or Braeburn.

1. Grate rind from lemon and set rind aside.

2. Squeeze juice from the lemon into medium bowl. Peel and core apples and cut into quarters. Dip apple pieces in lemon juice so they won't turn brown as you work with them.

3. Preheat oven to 350°F. Grease a 10-inch springform pan.

4. In medium bowl, combine flour and baking powder. In a large bowl, cream together butter and ½ c. sugar. Add eggs and lemon rind and blend until fluffy. Add flour mixture, mix well, and pour into pan.

5. Make deep lengthwise cuts in ⅛-inch intervals across rounded side of each piece of apple. Press apples, cut side up, into the dough.

6. In a small bowl, combine cinnamon with 2 tbsp. sugar. Sprinkle evenly over apples.

7. Bake for 30 to 40 minutes, or until toothpick inserted in center of cake (not in apple) comes out clean.

8. Serve with whipped cream.

Preparation time: 25 minutes
Baking time: 30 to 40 minutes
Makes 8 to 10 pieces

Butter Cookies / *Fränkische Butterplätzchen*

If you don't have cookie cutters, you can use a glass to cut out the cookies. This dough works well for holiday cookies cut in stars, bells, or hearts and decorated with colored icing.

½ lb. (1 c.) butter, softened

1 c. sugar

3 eggs at room temperature

½ tsp. vanilla extract

4 c. all-purpose flour

1. Beat butter, sugar, eggs, and vanilla in large bowl with electric mixer, or mix with spoon.

2. Set aside about 2 tbsp. of the flour to dust surface for rolling and rolling pin. Add flour, little by little, stirring well after each addition until all flour has been added and dough is smooth.

3. Preheat oven to 375°F.

4. Divide dough into thirds. Place one-third on a clean flat surface that has been dusted lightly with flour. Dust a rolling pin with flour and roll out the dough to ¼-inch thickness. Cut dough into a variety of shapes with cookie cutters that have been dipped in flour. Repeat with other two sections of dough. If necessary, dust rolling surface and rolling pin with flour again.

5. After cutting cookies from the three portions of dough, gather up leftover scraps of dough and roll into a ball. Reroll and cut more cookies.

6. Carefully place cookie shapes on ungreased baking sheets.* Bake 8 to 10 minutes, or until edges of cookies just begin to brown.

7. Cool baked cookies on a wire rack. Store these crisp cookies in a container with a loose lid.

Preparation time: 25 to 30 minutes
Baking time: 8 to 10 minutes per baking sheet
Makes 4 to 5 dozen

*For easier transfer of unbaked cookies to the baking sheet,
put a sheet of kitchen parchment paper on the sheet before arranging
the cut-out dough. After baking, just lift paper holding cookies
from the baking sheet to the cooling rack.

Holiday and Festival Food

Just as every Christmas stollen has lots of fruit, so every month of the German year has lots of holidays and festivals. A whole book could easily be devoted to the special foods that are served on special days of the year. For example, Twelfth Night, or Three Kings Day, is celebrated January 6. That day many people enjoy Three Kings Bread, a rich sweet bread crusted with sugar and nuts. The baker puts a single almond into each loaf, and the lucky person whose slice includes the almond can expect a year of good luck. There is always a party with favorite festive food to celebrate Carnival, the time just before Lent when children dress up in costumes. Holy (or Maundy) Thursday, the day before Good Friday, is called Green Thursday. Families have spinach soup garnished with hard-cooked eggs, or a creamy green soup made with spring herbs. May Day, May 1, is the time for dancing around the Maypole and having a picnic. Saint Martin's Day comes along November 11. Since Saint Martin is the patron saint of geese, drinking, and merrymaking, a fat goose is roasted and served with red cabbage or kraut and dumplings. And so it goes, through the year.

Marzipan candies are just as appetizing as they are fun to create.

New Year's Pork and Kraut/ *Schlachtplatte*

Bavarians usually plan to eat pork with sauerkraut the first day of the year—they believe this will prevent their running out of money during the new year. German cooks may use four or five different meats in this dish: ham, bacon, frankfurters, pork spareribs, pork shoulder roll, or whatever the family prefers. Boiled or mashed potatoes are a good accompaniment.

32-oz. jar sauerkraut

2 apples

I tbsp. oil , margarine, or vegetable shortening

I onion, chopped (I c.)

I c. apple juice or apple cider

2 boneless smoked pork chops (½ lb.), cut into 4 chunks

3 smoked pork bratwurst (½ lb.), cut into 6 slices each

2 tbsp. brown sugar

1. Put sauerkraut into a colander. Rinse under cold running water. Set aside to drain.

2. Peel and core apples, and cut into chunks. Heat oil in large kettle. Add onions and cook in oil until tender.

3. Squeeze excess water out of kraut using the back of a large spoon. Add kraut to kettle, stirring into onion.

4. Add apple juice, cut-up pork chops, and sliced bratwurst to kettle. Sprinkle in brown sugar. Mix well.

5. Cover kettle. Cook over low heat for 1½ hours, stirring occasionally.

Preparation time: 20 to 25 minutes
Cooking time: 1 hour 45 minutes
Serves 4 to 5

Peppernut Cookies / *Pfeffernusse*

Make these flavorful little cookies well ahead of the holiday season so that they can mellow.

¼ lb. (½ c.) butter or margarine, at room temperature

¾ c. packed brown sugar

1 egg

½ c. dark or light molasses

2⅓ c. all-purpose flour

1 tsp. cinnamon

½ tsp. baking soda

½ tsp. black pepper

½ tsp. ground nutmeg

½ tsp. ground cloves

¼ tsp. salt

1. In large mixing bowl, beat butter, sugar, egg, and molasses with electric mixer until smooth, or mix with spoon.

2. On a piece of waxed paper, stir together flour, cinnamon, baking soda, black pepper, nutmeg, cloves, and salt. Add flour mixture to bowl. Stir in flour mixture.

3. Turn the dough out on a lightly floured surface. Knead until a good consistency for shaping. If dough seems too soft to shape easily, refrigerate until firm.

4. Heat oven to 350°F. On a floured surface, roll one quarter of the dough into a long roll about 1 inch in diameter. Using a sharp knife, cut the roll into ¼-inch slices. Roll each slice into a little ball. Place in rows on a greased baking sheet.

5. Bake until set and golden brown on bottom, 8 to 10 minutes. Cookies harden on standing.

6. Store cool cookies in an airtight container with a slice of apple to mellow them.

Preparation time: 30 to 40 minutes
Baking time: 30 to 40 minutes
Makes 8 dozen

Easter Manikins / Ostermännchen

This holiday bread from the Rhineland delights little children.

1-lb. frozen sweet dough loaf, thawed but still cold

4 hard-cooked medium eggs, unpeeled (see directions on page 46)

milk for brushing dough

currants and slivered almonds for faces

1. Thaw dough according to package. Divide into four equal parts.

2. Working with one piece, pinch off about one-third. Shape half of this piece into a ball for the head. Shape other half into a rope for arms. Shape the other two-thirds of the piece of dough into a 4-in. long roll for body. Place roll for body on greased baking sheet. Press hard-cooked egg into upper portion of body. Place a rope of dough arms around egg. Attach head. With scissors or sharp knife, cut the lower part of body to form legs, and separate legs. Repeat with remaining dough and eggs.

3. Cover manikins. Let rise in warm place until doubled in bulk, about 30 minutes. Brush well with milk.

4. Heat oven to 375°F. Bake manikins for 10 minutes.

5. Remove from oven. Quickly add currant eyes and mouth and a slivered almond nose. Return to oven for 5 more minutes, or until golden brown.

Preparation time: 30 to 40 minutes
(plus rising time of 30 minutes)
Baking time: 15 to 18 minutes
Serves 4

Christmas Sweet Bread/ *Christstollen*

16-oz. package hot-roll mix

2 tbsp. sugar

1 c. hot water (120°F to 130°F, or very hot to touch)

1 egg, at room temperature

2 tbsp. butter or margarine, softened

½ tsp. ground cardamom (optional)

½ tsp. ground nutmeg

½ c. golden raisins

½ c. currants

½ c. cut-up candied cherries

flour for kneading

1 c. sifted powdered sugar

2 tbsp. whole milk or half-and-half

1. In large bowl, combine the hot-roll mix with sugar. Mix well.

2. Stir in hot water, egg, butter, cardamom, and nutmeg. Stir until dough pulls away from sides of bowl. Add raisins, currants, and cherries. Mix well.

3. Lightly sprinkle a work surface with flour. Turn dough out onto flour and knead for 5 minutes. Cover dough with a large bowl and let rest for 5 minutes.

4. Using a lightly-floured rolling pin, roll dough into an oval, 10 to 12 inches long and about 1 inch thick. Fold in half, cover, and let rise until doubled in bulk, about 45 minutes.

5. Heat oven to 375°F. Bake bread 22 to 25 minutes. If bread begins to brown too quickly, lay a piece of foil loosely over top. Bread is done when it is golden brown and sounds hollow when tapped.

6. Cool bread on a wire rack. Make icing by stirring together the powdered sugar and milk. Drizzle over cooled bread. Slice to serve.

Preparation time: 25 to 30 minutes
Rising time: 45 minutes
Baking time: 22 to 25 minutes
Makes 12 to 15 slices

Marzipan

Germany's finest contribution to the art of candy making is marzipan. This sweet almond paste mixture, shaped into figures, fruits, and vegetables, is a part of holiday celebrations. Marzipan fruits are typical for both Christmas and Easter. At Easter the candy is also shaped into bunnies and eggs.

8-oz. tube marzipan

paste colors or liquid food coloring*

cocoa powder or ground cinnamon, mint candies, and toothpicks for decorating candies

¼ c. light corn syrup diluted with 1 tbsp. hot water (optional)

*Paste color makes bright colors while liquid food coloring produces light colors.

1. Think of your favorite fruits and vegetables. Decide which four you want to make out of marzipan. Oranges, apples, potatoes, and tomatoes work well because they are basic round shapes. Strawberries, pears, and bananas can easily be molded out of marzipan too.

2. Wash your hands thoroughly, being sure to wash the backs of your hands and under your nails. Set up a work space at a table or kitchen counter and cover it with a cloth or kitchen parchment paper. Divide the marzipan into four equal parts of about 2 ounces each.

3. Use a small bowl for each color. Add desired color to marzipan and mix well. You could tint one part red for apples or tomatoes. Another part could be yellow for pears or bananas. Or, shape peas in the pod using green-tinted marzipan. Leave the other two parts the natural tan of the marzipan and apply color with a watercolor brush or simply by rolling the candy in a powdered ingredient such as cocoa.

4. Divide marzipan into 2-teaspoon clumps. Red apples or tomatoes would be an easy shape to start with. If you wish, you can add stems with bits of green mint candies.

5. Another easy shape is potatoes. Make them from untinted marzipan and roll in cocoa or cinnamon for the mottled brown outside. Use a toothpick to shape a few eyes in the sides of the potatoes. It's also easy to make strawberries since they are a rounded heart shape. Make dots all over the berries with a toothpick to resemble strawberries' texture. Take your time and use your imagination in forming the candies.

6. Let shapes stand uncovered for several hours. If you wish to glaze them, brush them with mixture of corn syrup and water. After glazing, let stand several hours, or until glaze is set.

Preparation time: 1 hour
Standing time: *several hours*
Glaze drying time: *several hours*
Makes about 12 candies

Index

About the Author

Helga Parnell grew up in the small town of Bamberg in western Germany. She moved to Saint Paul, Minnesota, in 1963. For many years she has managed the catering, food service, and gift shop for the German-American Institute, a German culture club in Saint Paul. Besides cooking, Parnell enjoys music, swimming, cross-country skiing, and teaching young children the customs and language of her native land. She lives with her husband in Mendota Heights, Minnesota.

Photo Acknowledgments
The photographs in this book are reproduced courtesy of: © B. Turner/TRIP, pp. 2–3; © Walter and Louiseann Pietrowicz/September 8th Stock, pp. 4 (both), 5 (both), 6, 16, 28, 35, 36, 41, 42, 44, 49, 52, 57, 60, 65, 66; © TH-Foto Werbung/TRIP, p. 10; © AFP/CORBIS, p. 12; © B. Gadsby/TRIP, p. 14; © F. Lulinski/TRIP, p. 24.

Cover photos: © Dave G. Houser/CORBIS, front (top); © Walter and Louiseann Pietrowicz/September 8th Stock, front (bottom), spine and back.

The illustrations on pages 7, 17, 25, 29, 33, 39, 40, 43, 45, 46, 47, 48, 51, 53, 56, 59, 61, and 68 and the map on page 8 are by Tim Seeley.